✺ ✺ ★ ✚ ★ ✺ ✺

The Blonde

Who

Found Jesus

By

Daveda Gruber

ISBN: 978-0-6152-2198-4

This book is dedicated

to

My husband, Sonny

Forward

This is Daveda Gruber's fourth book of poetry. Born in Montreal, Canada, Daveda now makes her home in the United States. Married to an American, destiny has led her to a new domain. Daveda loves the U.S.A. and proudly flies the American flag outside her home.

An animal lover all her life, Daveda loves her tiny Teacup Poodle named Lady Godiva. Appropriately, Lady Godiva has her own children's book which wins the hearts of the young and young at heart.

Daveda admits that she sometimes sees life a little differently than other people. She calls it a "Blonde View" of life. Her books have humor entwined in true life experiences. Having had her fair share of grief and difficult experiences she still comes through with a zest for living!

Daveda will proudly tell you that finding Jesus has kept her happy and lets her live a life filled with forgiveness and love for mankind. Step inside Daveda's "Blonde World" and join her as she graciously shares her love of Jesus in a way you have never experienced before.

Acknowledgements

To God and the Angels who watch over
me through good and bad times.
without my faith in Jesus,
I would not be here.

Special thanks to my friend and partner

Patricia Ann Farnsworth- Simpson
For

Professional

COVER DESIGN

**And the
extra help where needed**

Table of Contents

Table of Contents

I hope you enjoy my book!

God Bless,

Daveda

🕊 ✺ ★ ✚ ★ ✺ 🕊

The Blonde Who Found Jesus

Yes, I am the blonde who found Jesus.
I changed when I saw beauty of light.
His love is what He shines down to save,
All of those just like me in His sight.

~~*~~

If a Blonde like me can find Jesus;
Then there is still hope for all of you.
Remember, when found, all that has past,
Is gone, because Jesus makes life new!

~*~

The Dark Night

The night was black, no moon in sight.
We were in for a spooky night.
Don't step an inch, it could be bad.
I think I may be going mad.

~~*~~

Such darkness I have never seen.
It was starting to make me mean.
"Hello there" I heard myself say.
"Is anyone here out my way?"

~~*~~

Only an echo of myself,
Not easy to be with oneself.
How long can I stand in one place?
I felt my heart begin to race.

~~*~~

I moved my head; nothing was there,
Only the feeling of the air.
Do I dare sit on the cold ground?
If I wait here will I be found?

~~*~~

The night was black no moon it sight.
The earth pulled me; this was my plight.
Deeper and deeper I sank in,
The ground was nearly at my chin!

~~*~~

I could not move my limbs at all,
With no one near to hear my call.
I won't be able survive,
I surely cannot stay alive.

~~*~~

As I started to try to cry,
No sound, just a tear in my eye.
I need to be saved, but by who?
My mind has not even a clue.

~~*~~

Wild thoughts are going through my head.
My future I begin to dread.
Another thought enters instead,
Is it possible I am dead?

~~*~~

The night was black, no moon in sight.
I tried to think with all my might.
I remembered going to sleep.
I thought of the treasures I'd keep.

~~*~~

No cares in the world for others,
Snuggling under my covers.
Forgetting the sick and the weak;
They gave me no reason to speak.

~~*~~

The lonely had nothing for me,
Cared not for those who could not see.
Why would I save a friend in need?
All I knew in life was my greed.

~~*~~

I peeked from under my cover,
My life had much to discover.
I knew there was much to be done.
Good in me had finally won!

~*~

Guidance

At times I feel my life has gone insane,
Entangled with confusion in my brain.
I search inside, and see my strength now weak.
I do know, through Him, guidance I can seek.

~~*~~

For right now, too many things going wrong.
I ask you, dear God, where do I belong?
I ask, how much more torment can one take;
As much as you took, my Lord, for my sake?

~~*~~

Thank you Jesus, for showing me the light;
I see now that I can withstand my plight.
I thank you my Lord for what you've given;
So that, even I, can be forgiven.

~*~

🕊 ✺ ★ ✚ ★ ✺ 🕊

Raging Fire (Daveda's Cascade)

Tranquility is my desire;
Cannot exist with raging fire.
How many times must I forgive?
With constant fears how can I live?

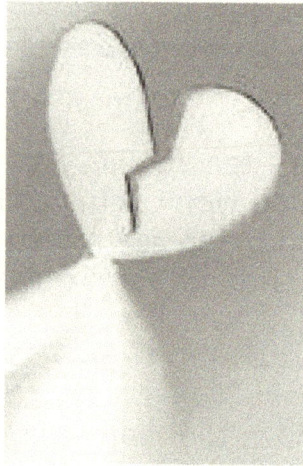

Essential for this heart is love.
I request from you, Lord above.
Quiet and peace I do require;
Tranquility is my desire.

~~*~~

It gets more difficult with time,
As I'm no longer in my prime.
I need your guidance to inspire;
Cannot exist with raging fire.

~~*~~

✌ ✺ ★ ✚ ★ ✺ ✌

Please help me Lord; to understand.
I am desperate; hold my hand.
The time past, is not to relive.
How many times must I forgive?

This weary heart has suffered pain.
More anguish will drive me insane.
There is much love I long to give,
With constant fears how can I live?

~*~

*Author's note: Cascade: a poem with an eight syllable
count ...the first stanza repeats itself as the ending line
in the following stanzas ...there is no rhyme required
but I have added rhyme to make it "Daveda's Cascade"

17

From Where I Came

I stand before you my Lord, once again.
My heart has trouble dealing with such strain.
The road gets smooth, but turns to bumps once more.
My travels take me where I was before.

†

Hopes and dreams to move forward are pushed back;
The strength to withstand this, I surly lack.
My mind is tiring of this foolish game.
Is it time to return from where I came?

†

Have new beginnings become my life's plan?
I fear that is the way my past began.
Has the sign been shown, but I do not see?
Maybe I've lost my opportunity!

†

May I walk with you, so that you may guide?
Right now, I need to be by your side.
I will do your bidding, just let me know.
Give me the direction and I will go.

†

🕊 ✳ ★ ✚ ★ ✳ 🕊

Please Hold My Daughter

(in memory of Lanie 1968-2004)

Sweet child of mine, another year has past.
Tiny teardrops and gushes of water
Have almost drowned me, in the pools so vast.
I miss your smile and laughter, my daughter.

~~*~~

I still dread the memory of that day.
The horrible sound of the phone ringing;
A voice brought the dreadful message my way;
A knife through my heart, which is still stinging.

~~*~~

A life gone without anything to gain,
On the day of her death she was confused.
A life with such unnecessary pain;
She suffered because she had been abused.

~~*~~

Lanie, can you hear your mommy crying?
I did all I could to help you, my child.
Was the only way out through you dying?
During your short life, had too much compiled?

~~*~~

My Lord and Savior, please hold my daughter.
Tell her that her Mommy still loves her so.
I can see her through my tears of water.
I will meet her again, please let her know.

~*~

Daughter in Heaven

for Lanie ...(November 18,1968 - January 9, 2004)

I lost a most precious part of me;
She lives in heaven, now she is free,
From the pain she suffered in her life.
At least I know she feels no more strife.

~~^~~

Although her body lies in a grave,
I know I must be strong and brave.
It hurts I cannot travel to her.
To give her flowers, I would prefer

.
~~^~~

She lived with me, for her last two years.
I tried to conquer her greatest fears.
Her dad had abused me years ago;
With that fact, she had to live and grow.

~~^~~

As she experienced my divorce,
More cruelty came to her with force.
Her dad said, that I now hated her,
Such terrible things did then occur.

~~^~~

Born two days before I was eighteen,
A child so close to me was a dream.
More like friends, than mother and daughter,
Same zodiac sign, we loved water.

Lanie enjoyed the life of the sea,
To me, that is an important key.
Whenever I see the dolphins play,
I feel Lanie close to me all day.

~~^~~

Butterflies made her smile, she would boast.
She loved fancy purple ones the most.
When I see a purple butterfly,
My heart lifts as I gaze to the sky.

Though in heaven my daughter now lives,
Her contagious laughter, she still gives
A video of her is my gift.
With her laughter, spirits she did lift.

My beautiful daughter, rest in peace,
My tears for you will not ever cease.
I will never stop loving you so.
I pray dear daughter that you do know.

~^~

Two Angels

To my daughter Lanie and my sister Sharon
(Shari the lionhearted)

I hear angel voices, loud and clear.
A beautiful sound, when they come near.
They sing songs, that put me in a trance,
To some answers, I'm given a glance.

~~*~~

I wonder, were some things meant to be?
I think they could be, to some degree.
My sister's body was never found;
She was not laid to rest in the ground.

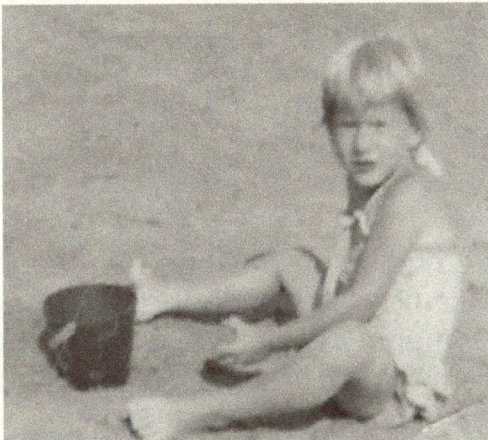

I felt that she was floating in space,
She was not resting in her own place.
I believe that spirits can be lost.
Sometimes, they do have their bearings crossed.

~~*~~

I never imagined what would be,
It was kind of strange, don't you agree?
While in a cemetery visiting,
Flowers for my father, we did bring.

Lanie had made clear to me that time,
"Sharon has no grave; I will share mine!"
She showed me the stone that she wanted;
Surprisingly, I was not daunted.

~~*~~

The day did come, when my daughter died.
Lanie was then buried and I cried.
Somehow I knew, she was not alone,
From a gust of wind, Sharon was blown

They were meant to be with each other,
One angel protecting another!
I hear angel voices, loud and clear.
A beautiful sound, when they come near

~*~

🕊 ✻ ★ ✚ ★ ✻ 🕊

Dear Daddy in Heaven

You told me that I was your special girl.
Over your head, you loved to make me swirl.
Late at night, you would let me watch TV.
On your lap, I loved it when you held me.

<<<>>>*<<<>>>

Daddy in Heaven, are you sleeping now?
As I hold back tears, I will not allow.
Daddy you told me, "Daveda don't cry,"
"For it has come the time that I must die."

<<<>>>*<<<>>>

Please Daddy; I cannot hold back my tears,
Even though it has been so many years.
I brought to life, more children, did you see?
Daddy, why is life still so hard on me?

<<<>>>*<<<>>>

So many times, I wished you were still here,
To take away all my troubles and fears.
Oh Daddy; all of the answers you had.
You knew how to make your little girl glad.

<<<>>>*<<<>>>

So, dear Daddy; I ask you to oversee,
Take care of my first child taken from me.
Also, watch over Sharon, my sister,
You understand, how much, I do miss her.

<<<>>>*<<<>>>

I have so many decisions to make.
My tattered heart will most certainly break.
From heaven, could you send me answers, please?
Dear Daddy, help my heart to be at ease.

<<>>*<<>>

🕊 ✺ ★ ✚ ★ ✺ 🕊

Sweet Sister

in memory of my sister ...Sharon ...
(Shari the lion-hearted)

Time of year keeps coming around again.
Imminent that there is approaching pain;
Sweet sister of mine your world was unkind.
An unused life and our love left behind.

~~*~~

Mom misses her baby; but grown up girl.
Wishes the story would one day unfurl;
Your death still holding so much mystery;
We have been told, now all is history.

Alive in your twenties, taken from us;
Police were not in the mood for such fuss.
Kept taking so long to investigate;
The deeds that ultimately sealed your fate.

~~*~~

April fools day is when you were taken;
You sleep in heaven with angels waken.
We will never know where your body lays;
Still taunting us and with our minds it plays.

I believe Jesus holds you in his arms,
Heaven, is where, He sees your lovely charms.
As an angel who watches over me,
In heaven; may your ambiance be free.

31

How Much Must I Learn?

I have experienced so much, I thought.
Yet, every time I think I know so much,
I realize it has not been a lot.
So, I move on, my destiny is such.

~~**~~

I am tired, but still cannot seem to sleep.
There is nothing to tell me what is next.
Yet, still in my heart, I want to just weep.
Love and hate mix together; so complex.

~~**~~

I desperately seek guidance from above.
The answers come back, to a confused mind.
After what has been done, why do I love?
Things have been evil and more than unkind.

~~**~~

All I want is to get on with my life.
I know that You; my Lord, are on my side.
I have tried so hard to be a good wife,
Why then every day and night, I have cried?

Ones Worth

I have met certain people along the road of life.
The ones that harbor hate in the depths of their soul,
Will be those who inevitably subsist with strife.
For they have permitted hatred to seize all control.

As they attempt to push forward into the future,
Their minds engulfed with judgments they can't explain.
While holding on to wicked thoughts that they nurture;
They uncaringly unleash insufferable pain.

~~*~~

Undeniable nasty thoughts are for the coward.
There is a much wiser way to survive on this earth.
To be able to forgive is to be empowered.
What one does for others will determine ones worth.

~*~

🕊 ✳ ★ ✛ ★ ✳ 🕊

Who Is Near?

I went to bed with much too much on my mind.
Too much confusion, answers I could not find.
I had been hearing three knocks each night I slept.
The number three; in my head, the question I kept.

I called out, "Daddy where are you, I need you!"
"My angels, Sharon and Lanie help me too!"
As I drifted off to into slumber, tears fell.
One, two, three, the knocks I could hear, where I dwell

I sat up in bed; then quickly checked the house.
No one there except my dog and a sleeping spouse.
I put my head on the pillow; closed my eyes,
Felt pressing on my mattress, to my surprise.

~~~*~~~

I questioned, "Who is here near me, on my bed?"
"Is this real, is someone here, or am I dead?"
A gentle soul slowly lay down, close to me.
Comforting arms held me, He said, "don't you see?"

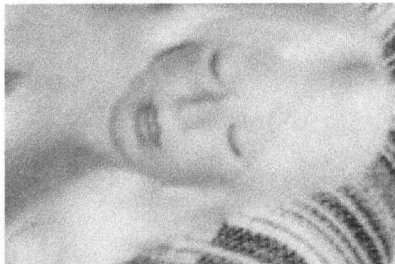

"I have come to say, all is well, stop to cry."
I felt a hug so unique; it made me sigh.
The face was one I felt trust in, from the start.
He was gone too fast, but remained in my heart.

~~~*~~~

I am prepared to be guided, by His love.
The visit I encountered came from above.
His kindness never ceases for those in need.
Have faith and know His words, you are meant to heed.

🕊 ✳ ★ ✚ ★ ✳ 🕊

The Kiss

For us, a moment in time, stood still.
Sweet music played in the distance;
A sacred vow, we would now fulfill.
Clearly, there would be no resistance.

I held his arm and was gently led.
Down the chapel path, love carried us.
From this moment on, we would be wed.
No words between us, left to discuss.

~~*~~

🕊 ❋ ★ ✚ ★ ❋ 🕊

The minister read from his pages,
As we gazed at each other, in bliss.
A love that would last through the ages,
Together, we had sealed with a kiss.

A reward that was long overdue;
Sensations felt; we were now content.
Aware we would forever be true;
From God in heaven, love had been sent.

~*~

Forgiveness

I stand before you, my Lord and savior.
Once again, we speak of my behavior.
I have asked for forgiveness, many times.
You can decipher between sins and crimes.

My dear Lord, who reigns on his throne above;
You must know my heart overflows with love.
I know I have stepped off the path of good.
I would gladly change my past, if I could.

My Lord, I know, you have forgiven me.
Still, there are others, who will not agree.
There are those who do not have a kind heart.
Their deeds can surely tear our lives apart.

My eyes filled with tears; that stream down my face.
Hateful words spoken cannot be erased.
My prayers, dear Jesus, are to help them see,
That to forgive another sets you free.

~*~

Faith (Double Etheree)

Faith
We need
More today
To keep us safe
In a troubled world
We must show Him our faith
That way He may help guide us
Knowing there is hope through the Lord
Let Him place you on the right path now
Have faith in God and give Him thanks each day

~~~~~ * * * * * ~ * ~ * ~ * * * * * ~~~~~

The Lord stays with you in all things you do
God loves you and cares for you each day
There are ways you can choose to live
The world without faith in God
Would not be the right choice
Place your heart with Him
God's love brings peace
To those who
Would have
Faith

🕊 ✻ ★ ✚ ★ ✻ 🕊

Colors by God (Haiku Suite)

shimmering crystals
floating down from the heavens
each unique in shape

clinging together
when falling in abundance
many become one

soft blanket of white
cooling earth's temperature
soil quietly sleeps

🕊 ✳ ★ ✚ ★ ✳ 🕊

snow caressed by sun
melting nourishing dry soil
seeds now arising

bursting forth fragrance
exquisite colors by God
new season begins

~*~

*Author's note Japanese Haiku nature is subject 5/7/5
syllable count ...poem relies on brevity

Hear Me (Rhyming Couplets)

Guidance is needed Dear Lord, please hear me.
I had two sisters, but one died you see.

Three children were raised by my loving heart.
My eldest child, from this world did depart.

A small family, I was born into.
I am living in a place that is new.

My dad is gone; my mom lives far from me.
New husband lives in a different city.

43

My husband's love is undoubtedly true.
Here all the people I meet are brand new.

~~*~~

I have been told my last sister will die;
More death coming makes my mom and me cry.

Dear Lord, by my husband's side, is my place.
I'll be the last child my mom can embrace.

My other children have hearts that are cold.
I hope that will change before I get old.

God, can you keep my last sister alive?
Please Jesus, give her more time to survive.

My heart is heavy; much too full of pain.
People are worse off; I should not complain.

45

The Road to Heaven (Double Etheree)

God
Father
Of Jesus
A friend to all
Taught us forgiveness
To share with everyone
Know of the power given
Never to hold hate in our hearts
In learning that love is the power
That has been given to each one of us

~~*<<<>>>*<<<>>>*~~

Eternity found through faith in our Lord
To love Jesus our channel to God
We are here for just a short time
Let's find the road to heaven
So our souls will find peace
He has the answers
We must trust Him
Show our faith
Give Him
Love

*author's note: Etheree 1st line 1 syllable 2nd line 2 syllables
...on till 10 syllables ...this is a double Etheree
...the 2nd one is reversed

Please Find a Cure

My doctor called with results from my test;
I was already nervous to find out.
He said, "Better come in; that will be best.
I will explain what all this is about"

~~*~~

I needed to know what was wrong with me.
Feeling bad news, as I rushed out the door,
The results were there; I needed to see.
Eyes on the doctor, I had to know more.

~~*~~

What I was told did not sound very good.
I had a disease which still has no cure.
This fact was apparent, I understood.
Details were plain of what I would endure.

~~*~~

Now, there is something certain which is clear.
It is others I must rely upon.
Knowing I can't help myself gives me fear.
Just research can help my problems be gone!

~*~

(This poem is fictional although for many it is real!)

It's Me Mom!

Did I have an appointment for my hair?
Where is it done and how do I get there?
Please tell me, it's so late, what shall I do?
Tell me your name; who am I talking to?

~~*~~

It's me mom, your daughter, I'm by your side.
Let's just you and me take a little ride.
We'll go to a nice place; you'll like it there.
There will be nurses who will give you care.

~~*~~

Mommy, don't cry; I'll visit every week.
Oh mom, I love the way you touch my cheek.
You're smiling, do you remember me now?
It's alright mommy, don't wrinkle your brow.

~~*~~

Sit down, mother, this chair is just for you.
This bed and pillows are yours; all brand new.
Mama, thank you, for hugging me so tight.
They'll find a cure; your future will be bright.

~*~

(another fictional poem, that is too real for so many)

A Prayer

Here I am again, asking Dear Lord.
Feelings of mine cannot be ignored.
A fine husband and wife need your love.
Please touch them with your hand from above.

Hank is quite sick and he needs our prayers,
Love for others; nothing else compares.
A wife needs her man to be alright.
Please Dear God; make this family's life bright.

Join me my friends; give a prayer today.
All is in God's hands, so let us pray.
Let's help Christina through this hard time.
With prayers, we can help Hank's hopes to climb.

(This poem was written for my friend and fellow poet
Christina R. Jussaume. Her husband was thought to have
cancer. Prayers have helped for the time being. He is being
closely monitored.)

49

God Is Here

My darling, have you no words to say?
Your once golden hair has tuned gray.
I look into eyes of azure blue.
It seems to be; I can see right through.

~~*~~

Can you see me, I am standing here?
Is it just as if, no one is near?
Do your ears know my voice, can you hear?
You have no answers; is what I fear.

~~*~~

Feel my tears dripping onto your face;
What do you do all day in this place?
Your face looks worn and tired today.
Shall we sit closely and try to pray?

~~*~~

My Lord and Savoir may I ask you;
Why is it that he forgot all he knew?
I have loved him for so many years;
Now, I cannot seem to stop my tears!

~~*~~

What is it honey, don't try to speak.
I listen to you; your voice is weak.
"God", yes sweetheart God is here with us.
Yes, my dear, it is He who will bless.

~~*~~

Please, say something else to me, my love.
You're pointing up to the sky above.
My dear sweet man, yes, that's where He is.
On the throne above, which is all His!

~~*~~

Please, my man who I love so dearly;
I could hear your voice, you spoke clearly.
Now your face is blank once more, to me.
Maybe I don't know how much you see!

~*~

(this poem is fictional for me, but not for many others)

🕊 ✳ ★ ✚ ★ ✳ 🕊

Gods Creations (Haiku Suite)

Clouds bright with color
hard to see sun shinning through
sky blazing like fire

orange combustion
ignites flames from God's Heaven
sun begins to set

cloud shapes start to form
God's creations empowered
bring beauty alive

moon slowly peeks through
fluffy clouds now dispersing
clear night now ahead

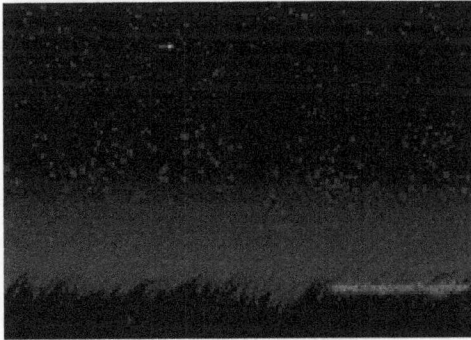

*Author's note: Japanese Haiku 5/7/5 syllable count ...poem
relies on brevity

I Believe in Angels

In memory of Lanie, my daughter, Sharon, my sister (Shari the lion-hearted) and Maxwell (my dad)

There are angels near; that I believe.
Yes, angels do help me, when I grieve.
My daughter is one, up in the sky.
I hear her wings, when I feel her fly.

My dear sister is an angel too.
She lives up in heaven; that is true.
Her body was never found on earth.
In heaven with God, she has much worth.

🕊 ✻ ★ ✚ ★ ✻ 🕊

Daddy lives up in heaven too.
They all have a very special view.
They all look down upon where I live,
Their protection to me, they all give.

Angels come in all different forms,
In good weather, and even through storms.
There are ones that cannot even fly;
They are friends who hear us, when we cry.

~*<>*~

🕊 ✳ ★ ✚ ★ ✳ 🕊

MY CHRISTMAS TRAY

Having some guests for Christmas this year,
Guests with different tastes I do fear.
I'll arrange a tray with assortment,
A fancy tray with lots of compartments.

~*~*~

Some mini hotdogs with a toothpick,
For little ones that will do the trick.
Tasty olives, the green and the black;
Those will be sure to make their lips smack.

Cold cuts rolled up; a pickle inside.
Now, that should make eyes open real wide.
Various variety of cheese,
That I could manage with so much ease.

~*~*~

Plenty of good wine both red and white,
Under the Christmas lights sparkling bright.
Some love and caring for everyone,
Now, it is starting to seem like fun.

My daughter will be spending time here
Now, that will make my heart sing with cheer.
My loving husband close by my side,
For him, I will be gleaming with pride.

~*~*~

With these things together on my tray,
Thinking of He, who was born this day.
Baby Jesus lay in a manger,
To grow up and become our savoir.

Happy New Year '09
(Acrostic-Senryu)

Having what we need
Harmony with peace of mind
Hopeful for others

A gift we received
Almighty is our Savior
Answers from above

Pride in believing
Prayers of thanks to be given
Power of His love

Praising one above
Preparing to move forward
Positive in thoughts

Years of past now gone
Yearning for better to come
Yielding from our fear

Not thinking badly
Never hurting with intent
New well wishes for future

Express decent thoughts
Effectively achieving
Everlasting love

Walking the right path
Where the future is unknown
Wishing for tranquility

🕊 ✳ ★ ✚ ★ ✳ 🕊

Yourself now finding
Yesterdays dreams coming true
Younger days now gone

Embracing His love
Embarking on the right road
Eternity ours

Asking approval
As we try to do our best
Achieving success

Ready to embrace
Reflections of Jesus' love
Redefining us.

*Author's note: this poem was written for my friend and fellow poet Christina's (crj147) challenge ...Acrostic/Senryu (Acrostic poem sends a message often with the 1st letter of each line) (Senryu 5/7/5 syllable count about God or human nature ...brevity is used)
Happy New Year!

Give Praise
(Candlelight)

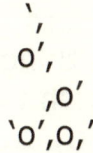

```
   `
    '
     /
  o',
    ,o'
`o',o,'
```
When you feel alone
You should not postpone
Give praise to His name
Know that He came
To teach His word
Hope you heard
They cried
He died
For you
And
Me
So
He
Is
With
Us
Each and every day we live

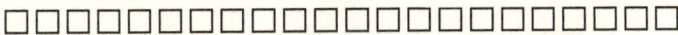

□□□□□□□□□□□□□□□□□□□□□□□□

*Author's note: Candlelight was created By Christina R Jussaume 12/03/07

Jesus I Pray

Faith, in our Lord Jesus, can be strong.
Still, we see that things can go right or wrong.
At times, I wish to throw in the towel.
My voice tones may start to sound like a growl.

I see much negativity so close.
Times when I feel I am trying the most.
Belief that the day is going so fine,
Then, thoughts generate sentiments malign.

~~**~~

Dear Lord, I plea for your intervention;
Could really use some of your attention.
Just hear my side of our conversation;
Jesus, I must give you information.

Many have died who were so close to me.
Are they with you Lord, I wish I could see.
From the beginning my family was small.
Through the years, I witnessed as more did fall.

~~**~~

~~**~~

Knowing there is uncaring, what a mess.
I live far away; so there is much stress.
I have not many friends here to speak of!
Lord, only a small few are full of love.

~~**~~

I am strong; I believe God is with me.
I know that my Lord Jesus is the key.
Jesus, I pray to you for some insight.
Please, help me to get through, just one more night.

✌ ❋ ★ ✚ ★ ❋ ✌

Choosing His Way
(an Easter poem)

A man who had helped and healed so many,
In fact, He would never deny any.
A tribunal did not believe his views.
Pontius Pilot called him King of the Jews.

This gentle man was whipped till his blood flowed.
On Him, a painful crown of thorns, bestowed.
They kicked him and gave Him terrible pain,
For no real reason, that they could explain.

***

To Cavalry He carried His own cross.
Such pain already, still stones they did toss.
Nails were hammered into His hands and feet.
Thinking, His will, they could fully defeat.

🕊 ✳ ✦ ✚ ✦ ✳ 🕊

The man dying on the cross proved His cause,
He showed forgiveness, to those who had flaws.
He suffered for those who did and still sin.
Love Him and give praise and glory to Him.

It took many hours before pronounced dead.
His disciples knew not what lay ahead,
Until he rose to spread his word to us.
In hopes we would always give Him our trust.

Give praise to Him, who was not, but a man;
The Son of God had in His heart, a plan.
Show your love for Him by choosing His way.
Then, shall you be with him, on judgment day.

*10 syllable rhyme "10" (for I believe Jesus is a 10!)

Happy Easter (Acrostic-Rhymed)

Heaven is where He lives.
All of Himself He gives.
Prayers He listens to, each day.
Praise Him and live His way.
You will find joy in your heart.

Easter tells he did never depart.
Assuring us there was a plan.
Son of God He was, not a man.
Through His labor of love,
Eternity is what we learn of;
Reminding us, he is waiting above.

Needing You Near (Ottava Rima)

It is me again Dear Lord, needing You near.

My mother's voice sounds weaker when I call;

She is feeling that death is close, I fear.

Without her, my family becomes small.

How many more times must I shed a tear?

My sister is not able to stand tall.

Lord Jesus my only feelings are sad.

Right now, my world seems to be going mad.

*Authors note:
Ottava Rima: 8 lines 10 syllables per line ...rhyme scheme
a,b,a,b,a,b,c,c

God Takes Care of You
(Rhyming Couplets)

I brought you chocolates for Valentine's Day.
Mom, I thought also, maybe we could pray.

Knowing you get confused about some things;
We can thank God for the good that He brings.

~~*~~

You eat good food and have a nice clean bed.
So, let us thank God for our daily bread.

~~*~~

The flowers in the garden are in bloom;
Lovely for you to smell, like fine perfume.

~~*~~

❀ ✿ ★ ✚ ★ ✿ ❀

We can thank God every day for the beautiful sky;
Sun and moon amongst fluffy clouds we cannot deny.

~~*~~

Mommy, I know God takes care of you,
I feel that Jesus loves us both too.

~~*~~

One day we will both be in His arms.
Then, once again, I will see your charms.

My Valentine's wish is you are alright here.
Deep within my heart, I know you have no fear.

~*~

🕊 ✺ ✦ ✚ ✦ ✺ 🕊

Ever in Awe (Daveda's Charm)

Preparing to love
Remembering Him above
Ever in awe of

~*~

Certain of the way
It can be hard not to stray
Offer praise today

~*~

Use what He has shown
Sharing the gift that is known
Lord sits on His throne

~*~

As faith becomes strong
Do what is right and not wrong
Your joy will be long

🕊 ✹ ★ ✚ ★ ✹ 🕊

Destiny is to be your guide;
As you love Him with so much pride.
Victory is love He provides.
Elevating you, with great strides.
Decide to live your life His way,
As you learn each day when you pray;
`

Sacrifices He made for you.

~*~

Cherish the fact that Jesus knew
How hard it is to have no sin.
A good thought for you to begin;
Remembering we must forgive,
Making it possible to live.

*Authors note "Davedas Charm" ... a poetry form created by
Christina R Jussaume on 03 24, 2008.It begins with 4 senyru
that begin with the letters P R E C I O U S L A D Y. This is
followed by two acrostics in 8 syllable count. The acrostics
must begin with the letters D A V E D A' S and the next
stanza C H A R M. I have not used rhyme, but it is an
option. This form I have created as a tribute to a special poet
friend, Daveda Gruber. Subject should be uplifting.

It Won't Get Me!

One day in the cold month of November,
No way that I could ever remember;
Many rejoiced as love flowed out to me.
Wishes, a good woman; one day I'd be.

~~*~~

The roads chosen have not always been right,
When it was needed, I fought the good fight.
As my trails of life began to get rough,
I answered with all my strength and got tough.

~~*~~

🕊 ✳ ★ ✚ ★ ✳ 🕊

When my tears flowed like rivers, as I cried,
I wiped them quickly, that can't be denied.
From what is thrown at me, I will not hide.
The strength that is needed, God will provide.

~~*~~

If this new battle tries to bring me down,
I won't permit weakness to be around.
This darn test with its results won't get me.
I'll fight to the end; that I guarantee!

*author's note ...I had a serious test scheduled ...the results
could have changed my life ...my faith got me through it
I am fine now

🕊 ✳ ✦ ✚ ✦ ✳ 🕊

Time is Now (Christina's View)

Christian way is just right for me.
His love for us will set us free.
Righteous life is right you will see.

~~*~~

Inner love for almighty one,
Start now, if you have not begun.
Time is now; give praise to God's Son.

~~*~~

🕊 ✹ ★ ✚ ★ ✹ 🕊

In your heart you know it is true;
Saviour of man, including you.
Salvation he extends anew.

~~*~~

Anyone who opens their heart,
Valuable love He will impart.
Is that not a wonderful start?

~~*~~

Ordinary Jesus was not,
Unifying us not forgot;
Remembering what Jesus taught!

~*~

*"Christina's View" ...poetic form created by Christina R
Jussaume on 04 03 08. It begins with five triplets in rhyme
of 8 syllable count. These triplets must start with the letters

C H R I S T....IS.....S A V I O U R.
Poem must be spiritual in nature.

In Force (Tanka Suite)

Ice scorches the earth
Winter has damaged pure soil
Seasons keep cycle

Chilling wind bites at small buds
Bitter frost clawing to stay

Frost has won for now
Wintry iciness still clings
Hope for change still waits

Morning sun brings warmth
Gentle breeze tenderly smiles

🕊 ✳ ★ ✚ ★ ✳ 🕊

Beauty uplifting
Beckons enticing flowers
Tiny bird feels safe

Danger lurks fulfils hunger
Nature's cycle still in force

~*~

***Author's note …Tanka 5,7,5,7,7 syllables … the best
tanka harmonizes the writer's emotional life with the
elements of the outer world used to portray it.**

✄ ❋ ★ ✚ ★ ❋ ✄

I Am A Chocolate Covered Cherry
to chocolate lovers everywhere...

I am a chocolate covered cherry, so sweet;
Seen through a glass case, my life just seems complete.
Many friends I have here; they giggle all the time.
I love my home in the case; life is so sublime.

~~<<<>>>~~

Some of my buddies are chocolate cherries, like me.
Others are different, but fun, I guarantee.
We see a tall blond man, looking over at us;
About buying chocolate, we hear him discuss.

~~<<<>>>~~

He says, "Just the cherries; put them in a box, please".
The lady asks, "Gift wrapped?" tall blond man agrees.
Wow, we are going to be a gift, we all smiled.
Who will we be a present for; our thoughts compiled.

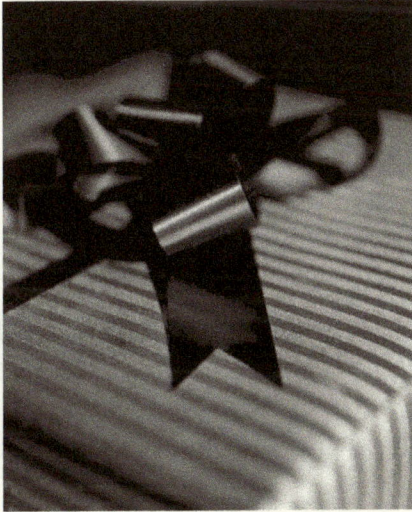

It was dark and spooky in that box, we agreed.
We are starting to get scared; we need to be freed.
A lovely blonde lady, has just unwrapped the box.
She is so beautiful; hey guys she is a fox!

Oh my, such soft hands and long nails, we can feel her.
"I love chocolate covered cherries", she does purr.
"I want to eat only two of them", she does state.
The tall blond guy puts eight of my friends, on a plate.

Oh, I feel fear for my life; please do not eat me!
"You eat too much chocolate; do you not agree?"
Then she explains, "Well, I will hide the rest of these".
She just puts us all away, with such expertise.

~~<<<>>>~~

For days, we are hidden away here, in a drawer.
No one seems to care about us; not anymore.
Oh wait; she wants a chocolate covered cherry.
"Where are my chocolates?" she asks, quite contrary.

"You ate them; I know you always eat chocolates!"
She wonders where he put her chocolates; she waits.
He searches far and wide, for the delicious treat.
So, what will be the outcome; what fate will we greet?

~~<<<>>>~~

She watches him closely, as he searches the house.
"I blame you, because you eat chocolate, my spouse!"
Yes, I do cry, he will eat us; I do despair!
He will eat and swallow me down whole; I declare!

She sits there thinking; a thought comes into her head.
"I hid them from you; and from myself; I do dread!"
She stands up; walks to the drawer in her night table.
"Here they are"; oh no, we are feeling unstable.

~~<<<>>>~~

🕊 ✳ ★ ✚ ★ ✳ 🕊

She opens the box; she takes us out of the dark.
I begin to shake; she could eat me, I remark.
I am scared, and I close my eyes as she touches me.
Oh no, she's putting me in her mouth; I can't see!

It is murky in here, but she has a soft tongue.
I am sliding; slipping down and I am so young.
What will happen now; I think it is time to pray.
Oh please dear God; I do need your help on this day.

Gates open; I am in chocolate heaven now.
I see so many of my old friends here; oh wow!
The moral to this story; is not very grim;
If you pray, you can have eternity with Him!

~<<>>~

🕊 ✳ ✦ ✚ ✦ ✳ 🕊

Think of Him
(Christ-in-a-Rhyme)

Easy to find; for He is near,
What he said was always sincere.
Open the bible; have no fear.

Such wisdom throughout His words are so effortless to see.
The road of life becomes complex for all in some degree.
Put burdens down He will pick them up and you will feel free.

Take Jesus into your heart;
Changes in your life will start.
Loving Him is very smart.

When the light seems dim,
Things seem to be grim.
Stop, and think of Him.

You know what to do;
His love is so true.
It's now up to you.

*author's note: Christ-in-a-Rhyme was created by
Christina R Jussaume

🕊 ✳ ★ ✚ ★ ✳ 🕊

The Power Within

There is a power
in the love you have for God
listen to His word

The
Power
Within you
Gives you the choice
If you choose the path
That He would be proud of
For He loves all of mankind
We are all the same in His eyes
He loves those who show love for others
Be kind and be good to your fellow man

^^*^*^*^*^*^*^*^*^*^*^*^*^*^*

You will feel joy in your heart when you give
Of yourself to those who need a friend
Open your heart and let love flow
Extend kindness to others
There is no greater gift
That you could offer
So Help to spread
This message
Of His
Love

꒰ ✻ ★ ✚ ★ ✻ ꒱

∧∧*∧*

He gives us His love
for His love has the power
to make us feel good

∧

*author's note 1st a senryu (about God or human nature
5/7/5 syllables) ...then a double etheree (1/2/3 till 10
syllables then reversed 10/9/8 till 1 syllable) ...ending with
another senryu

My Wealth

I'm lucky to have riches beyond belief,
Wealth shows through poet friends when I have grief.
As I cuddle my puppy, I feel much wealth.
Riches I have, through reasonably good health.

A lovely daughter, I have, who loves me so.
So many riches were gained, watching her grow.
I can call my mother and talk all the time.
She is in good health even though past her prime.

I have such riches inside this heart of mine.
Lovely memories bring a feeling so fine.
I love to help others, so that is a gift
If I make someone happy, I get a lift.

My wealth lets me send poems to a marine,
Although, his appearance to me is unseen.
I have a wealth of thoughts that go through my head.
That lets me write poetry, which I can spread.

The bulk of my wealth, which is a part of me,
Is something very special I cannot see.
My faith in God is within my inner soul.
Jesus, who guides me, does play the starring role.

~*~

Peace of Mind
(Double Etheree)

Peace
Of mind
I have found
In love of God
For He is with me
No matter where I am
Regardless of what I do
His love is the greatest of all
He guides me in doing what is right
I give thanks to God each and every day

~*~~*~*^*^*^*~*~*~*~*^*^*^*~*~*~

God will help you find peace and joy within
Have faith and take Him into your heart
Share with others the love you find
Such a simple thing to do
It will give joy to you
Happiness is yours
You can find it
Look to God
To find
Peace

🕊 ✺ ★ ✚ ★ ✺ 🕊

Love to Share
(Daveda's Dix-Par-Deux)

Surviving this life is not always kind.
Look up to heaven and open your mind.

My friends, just try, this is not hard to do.
Know in your heart; He's always there for you.

Looking...

🕊 ❋ ★ ✚ ★ ❋ 🕊

It's not difficult to find the right road.
A place awaits you to put down the load.

God picks up what is too heavy to bear.
Lighten your fear He understands despair.

Finding...

He has much love to share with all of us;
To those who believe his way; He will bless.

If you look you will find what is waiting;
Love for the son of God is elating.

Loving...

"Daveda's Dix-Par-Deux" is a new style of poetry invented
on 03/04/08 ...the style consists of 2 rhyming couplets of 10
syllables making up each line ...then a line of 2 syllables (the
2 syllable lines must sum up the 2 couplets they follow) ...2
more 10 syllable couplets and another line of 2 syllables
...you can do as many as you wish

My Faith
(French Ballade)

I have found a good way to be.
I love to go to Church and pray,
Being grateful, that I can see.
I look up and the sky is gray,
Still, I can have a pleasant day.
I believe that is so clever.
Good will towards others, I display.
My faith, I will keep, forever.

~~*~~

Forgiveness is part of the key.
Dire deeds will not stand in my way,
Even though you may disagree.
Learning there are ways to convey,
As I help others not to stray.
The good life is my endeavor.
You should listen to what I say.
My faith, I will keep, forever.

~~*~~

I feel that we should both agree,
Feeling close with God everyday,
Will award a way to feel free.
There is no reason to delay.
Take Jesus in your heart, today.
He will guide you right, whatever.
He will never lead you astray.
My faith, I will keep, forever.

~~*~~

You so called Prince; to my dismay,
This relationship, I sever.
I suggest that you walk away.
My faith, I will keep, forever.

~*~

French Ballade: syllable count remains the same for each line (8)...3- 8-line stanzas rhyming ababbcbC, ...followed by a 4-line envoi rhyming bcbC ...the same rhymes being used throughout ...the upper case C's indicate that the same line is repeated at the end of each stanza ...these days, the envoi (last stanza that wraps up the poem) is addressed to Prince ...generally understood to be the Prince of Darkness

Road of Life

As I travel the road of life.
I recede to look at the strife.
For the places I have been to,
The hardships, which I have gone through,
Have shown to me the shinning light.
Good and bad, also wrong and right.

~~*~~

꙳ ✳ ★ ✚ ★ ✳ ꙳

A daughter was taken from me;
Now, trust in God is what I see.
My sister was murdered, I know,
Still, I must continue to grow.
Although her body was not found,
Never laid to rest in the ground.

~*~

Abuse is no stranger to me.
I have found the way to break free.
I will not hold hate in my heart;
To let it go; is to be smart.
Holding hate is for the coward.
Forgiveness makes you empowered.

~*~

*Author's note Abuse can come in different ways ...physical
and/or mental ...no matter how difficult life becomes ....to
hold hatred is negative energy ...forgiveness and love are
never a burden

✹ ✸ ★ ✚ ★ ✸ ✹

Bring Out the Mop
(Rhyming Couplets)

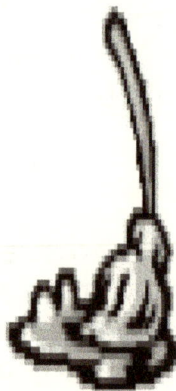

It seems sometimes things do not go my way.
I guess we all can have that sort of day.

~~***~~

My dear friends, try to give me good advice.
I feel thankful that others are so nice.

~~***~~

I have found when I have lost my wits.
There is something else to lift my spirits.

~~***~~

Whether or not I know, Jesus is here.
I must say, He sure helps me persevere.

~~***~~

🕊 ✸ ✮ ✚ ✮ ✸ 🕊

When I feel that the world is throwing slop;
It seems I must go and bring out the mop.

~~***~~

Life has always been, when one thing goes wrong;
Others seem to want to follow along.

~~***~~

I keep my faith focused on God above.
That way I can keep my heart full of love!

~*~

✿ ❋ ★ ✚ ★ ❋ ✿

A Songbird's Wings

Lord, I ask, please, show us the means to give;
So many of us loved Lela's sweet song.
We want to make Lela's memory live.
A songbird can continue to be strong.

~~*~~

We stand as a memory to our friend.
We dedicate a book to all who care;
In hopes that some hearts we can try to mend;
Or, if not, we can give hope to repair.

~~*~~

🕊 ✳ ★ ✚ ★ ✳ 🕊

Lela your sweet song we can hear above.
The ones who were enlightened by your dreams,
Know that songbird will continue to love;
From a songbird's wings pure radiance gleams.

🕊 ✴ ★ ✝ ★ ✴ 🕊

He Is There

When this tattered heart is devoid of all;
An ambiance of darkness cloaks my soul.
Crawling into myself, I feel so small;
Despair and concern; a need to be whole.

~~*~~

My eyes look up to the azure blue sky.
Closeness encompasses my entity.
A need, my Lord senses, in my sad cry.
He is aware of each identity.

~~*~~

Call to Him, He hears each and every prayer.
I can attest to the love He gives me,
Love Him, and feel certainty, He is there.
Open your eyes wide; gaze above and see.

~~*~~

Jesus my faith is stronger every day.
You ease my soul, when I am almost down.
My Lord, I give praise to you, as I pray.
Fears are lifted, knowing you are around!

~*~

His Way

The only perfection that I see;
Is not something seen in you or me.

I ask from above, the help I seek;
If not; this world will be awfully bleak.

~~*~~

Hope others can choose to live His way;
For this dear Lord, I look up and pray.

❧ ✻ ★ ✚ ★ ✻ ❧

If we can live on earth, and give love;
Just as He gives to us from above.

~~*~~

The world would be a much better place,
For all of us in the human race.

~*~

Love Survives
(Daveda's Dix-Par-Deux)

A bitter wintry day freezes the skin;
Frozen moments glimpsing at what has been.

Desperately clawing bits of what was;
Lost to memories of yesterdays cause.

Find me...

Warming glow burns beneath the frigid ice.
Turning back time will by no means entice.

Melting chilly frost piled high to cover;
Explore today and you'll rediscover.

Know me...

🕊 ✳ ★ ✚ ★ ✳ 🕊

Bonding as one, the path chosen by two;
Deeds approved as heaven above is blue.

Sharing faith; keeping it part of our lives.
Watching pure beauty as our love survives.

Love me...

"Daveda's Dix-Par-Deux" is a new style of poetry invented on 03/04/08 ...the style consists of 2 rhyming couplets of 10 syllables making up each line ...then a line of 2 syllables (the 2 syllable lines must sum up the 2 couplets they follow) ...2 more 10 syllable couplets and another line of 2 syllables ...you can do as many as you wish

Vessel of Love
(Spirit's Vessel)

Vessel of gentle love,
Expression from above;
Savoir of believers.
Selfless be receivers,
Exemplifying Him;
Light of God never dim.

Offer Him devotion,
Feeling good emotion,

You'll learn good way to live.
Offering love to give.
Uncovering within,
Reasons to let you win.

Let His light flow on you,
Open your heart and view.
Victory will be yours,
Ignited, your heart soars.
Nothing more elating;
God will be there waiting!

*This poetry form "Spirit's Vessel" was created by:
Christina R. Jussaume on 04 07 08. It consists of three
stanzas of six lines each of six syllables each.
These stanzas must start with the letters
VESSEL Of YOUR VERSE.
The poem must be spiritual or about God's gifts
and uplifting in nature.

☙ ✳ ★ ✚ ★ ✳ ☙

Would You Know Him?

If you saw a man wearing tattered clothes,
His shoes dirty from taking a long walk;
Would you show Him kindness and love that flows?
If He sat along the road, would you talk?

~~*~~

If He asked you to help a friend in need;
You knew there was nothing for you to gain.
Would you be happy to do a good deed?
Even if for you, it could be a strain?

~~*~~

Would you know the face of the son of God?
If He showed himself to you, would you see?
Now think, would this man just look very odd?
An ordinary man dressed so shabbily.

~~*~~

🕊 ✳ ★ ✚ ★ ✳ 🕊

Jesus never dressed in riches and lace.
He dressed like the poor who had loved him so.
Pilate condemned to death, a weathered face.
If He came to you, would you really know?

~*~

🕊 ✳ ★ ✚ ★ ✳ 🕊

Glowing Light
(Ottava Rima)

Grateful that God is close within my sight,
Faith has been my salvation; that I see.
If not for the warmth of His glowing light,
Which gave me the strength to set my heart free.
No fear of future, because all is bright.
When I need Him, He will be beside me.
He knows my honesty when I give praise.
I show Him by living life by His ways.

~*~

*Author's note Ottava Rima: 8 lines of 10 syllables per line
...Rhyme is a,b,a,b,a,b,c,c

Hello Lord Jesus
(Rhyming Couplets)

Hello Lord Jesus, please step inside.
You know that my door is open wide.

~~*~~

Always nice for you to visit me,
People are not always fair you see.

~~*~~

Why can they not stop being unkind?
Is the goodness in me, hard to find?

~~*~~

✶ ❋ ★ ✚ ★ ❋ ✶

Yes, Dear Lord, I see such love in you.
I know what you tell to me is true.

~~*~~

Mankind nailed you to a wooden cross;
Your mother cried for the greatest loss.

~~*~~

I complain about nothing at all;
Now, I feel ashamed and awfully small.

~~*~~

Once again, I was feeling alone;
You are with me Lord, I should have known.

~~*~~

Still, every time we have a small chat;
You leave me with a lot to smile at.

~*~

*author's note Rhyming Couplets ...each group of two lines
has the same syllable count and rhyme

✶ ✹ ★ ✚ ★ ✹ ✶

All is Bright
(Daveda's Dix-Par-Deux)

Through insight, life is easier to see;
Each wonderful day God has given me.

I do not dwell upon negative things;
Instead, noticing what good living brings.

Seeing...

The little things in my world do feel good;
Smiling with knowledge that is understood.

When the natural flow seems to be right,
Sensing the reality; all is bright.

Feeling...

Sure, the road of life has its ups and downs;
Still, there is no reason to see the frowns.

I have something that all of you could too;
Jesus is by my side in all I do!

Knowing...

~*~

"Daveda's Dix-Par-Deux" is a new style of poetry invented
on 03/04/08 ...the style consists of 2 rhyming couplets of 10
syllables making up each line ...then a line of 2 syllables (the
2 syllable lines must sum up the 2 couplets they follow) ...2
more 10 syllable couplets and another line of 2 syllables
...you can do as many as you wish!

✌ ✺ ★ ✚ ★ ✺ ✌

Other books by this author:

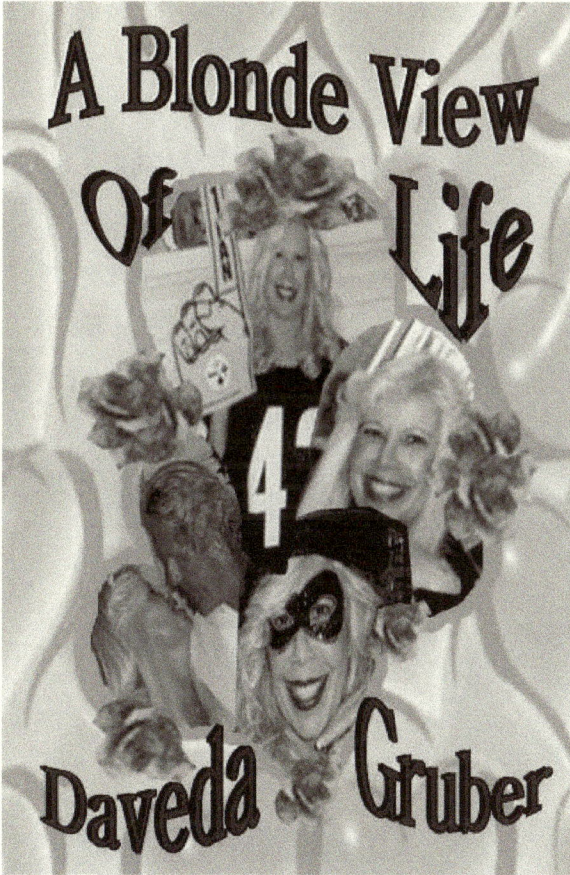

A Blonde View Of Life

Daveda Gruber

P.F.P Publishers

✶ ❋ ✭ ✚ ✭ ❋ ✶

Other books by this author:

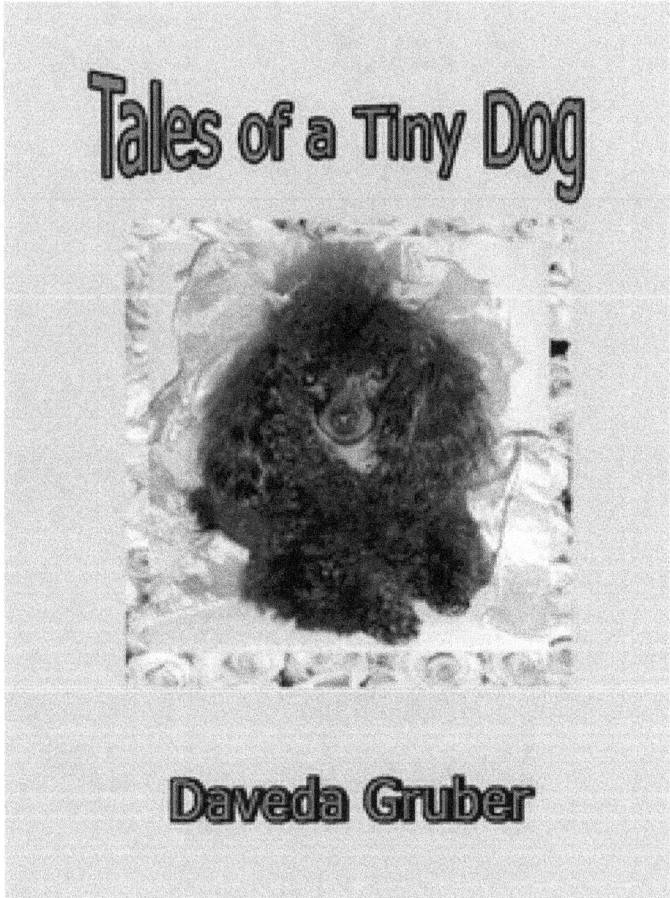

Tales of a Tiny Dog

Daveda Gruber

P.F.P Publishers

More books by this author:

Soul Asylum Publishers

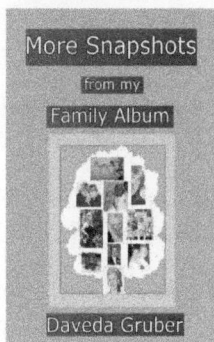

P.F.P. Publishers

Please visit my website at:

www.davedagruber.com

Windows of Light

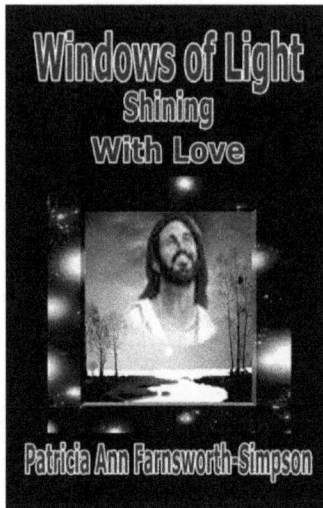

There are many good books to buy today,
One in particular has much to say.

Open the window that will give you light;
You'll find a world shining with love so bright.

Patricia Ann Farnsworth-Simpson is host,
To a certain book of which, I must boast.

Love of God and faith are what she will bring;
Give yourself a chance for your heart to sing.

The wonder of pictures she brings to life;
As a mother, grandmother and a wife.

Love of animals and friendship she gives.
All comes freely; it is the way Pat lives.

Buy a book that will keep bringing you back.
There is not a thing that this book does lack.

You will never regret the time you spend;
But, you'll want more when you come to the end.

~*~

Spiritual Living Waters

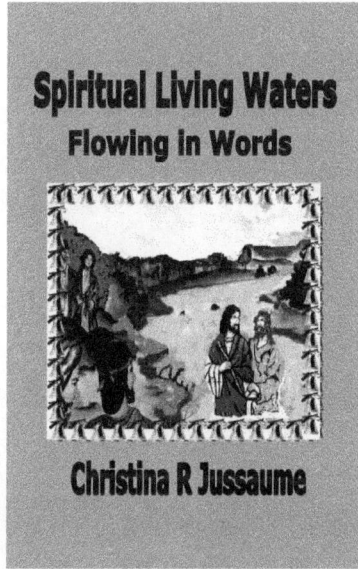

Spiritual Living Waters
Flowing in Words

Christina R Jussaume

Words flow from poetry at its best.
A poet with talent can do it.
Some are without doubt, above the rest.
Words from our Lord, Tina does commit.

"Spiritual Living Waters" tells,
A way to make life perfect for us.
Pride for the Lord Jesus always swells;
In Christina's books with much success.

Love for God is what she writes about.
Her family is first to agree;
In her life there is never a doubt.
God is first whatever comes to be.

Pictures of family can be seen;
Her poetry styles will draw you in.
Throughout a life with God is routine,
You'll feel the power of Christ within.

Take a walk with my friend Christina,
Her new book will teach to love The Lord;
You may just want to call her Tina.
Her book is an ultimate reward.

Other Books by P.F.P

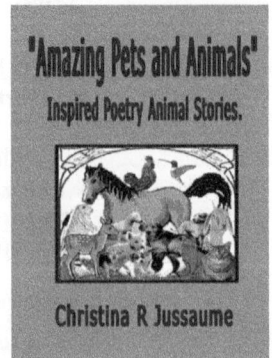

Spiritual Thoughts on Love & Life
Michael L Schuh

'But It's Mine' Says The Moon-Shiner
Michael L Schuh

'Choose The Right' and Walk With Noah
Richard A Rooney II

"Standing Tall" When Feeling Small
by Poet's World-Wide

'The Trojan Horse'
Erich J Goller

FAVORITE POEMS
GREAT POETS 2008

'Life's Carousel'

The Jester's Book Of Humorous Tales
POEMS JOKES
By POETS World-Wide

"Amazing Pets and Animals"
Inspired Poetry Animal Stories.
Christina R Jussaume

Other Books by P.F.P

Pieces of Existance

Joe Hartman

Born To Be a Rebel

Joanne Agee

www.ingramcontent.com/pod-product-compliance
Lightning Source LLC
Chambersburg PA
CBHW032105080426
42733CB00006B/422